HISTORY & TECHNIQUES OF THE

Great Masters

VAN GOGH

HISTORY & TECHNIQUES OF THE

Great Masters

VAN GOGH

William Hardy

CHARTWELL BOOKS, INC.

A QUANTUM BOOK

Published by Chartwell Books
A Division of Book Sales Inc.
114 Northfield Avenue
Edison, New Jersey 08837
USA

This edition printed 2003

ISBN 0-7858-1650-X

QUM1VAN

This book is produced by
Quantum Publishing Ltd.
6 Blundell Street
London N7 9BH

Printed in China by Leefung-Asco Printers Ltd.

Contents

Introduction

Vincent Van Gogh
Self-Portrait
1888
Van Gogh Museum, Otterlo

Vincent Van Gogh died by his own hand, an impoverished failure in the eyes of the world. He had struggled to succeed in a number of fields: as an art dealer, teacher, missionary and only finally as a painter. He committed suicide at the very time his work was beginning to attract both critical approval and the enthusiasm of his fellow artists, yet today he is probably the most popular and widely known painter in the entire history of art, known to millions through reproductions of his works. The contrast between the obscurity of his life and his universal posthumous acclaim has become in the popular imagination the prototype story of the modern artist: a poor and dejected outcast, descending into madness, but whose genius, inevitably only recognized after his early death, brings him immortality.

Van Gogh would not have despised this popularity, for above all else he wanted his painting to reach ordinary people and be a part of their lives. His great compassion for the suffering of others, together with the pain and loneliness he suffered himself, gave to his art a universality beyond dry intellectual or historical themes, and his life itself seemed to dramatize the very essence of the emotions that we all encounter, albeit less intensely. In this respect his paintings deal with things that are simple to recognize and easy to sympathize with, whatever our own particular experiences have been.

Not only do Van Gogh's paintings address fundamental human emotions very directly, they also depict the real world square on. His subject matter was nearly always what was before his easel — concrete, familiar, everyday reality. Although he was highly literate, deeply absorbed in spiritual issues and had a thorough knowledge of artistic tradition, his work is never complicated by obscure allusions or layers of meaning intelligible only to the few. Although his paintings have great depth, this is never at the expense of direct impact. The obvious sincerity of his work is one of its chief attractions, and its emotional force is very directly conveyed through his painting technique. His brushwork is almost a form of speech, and a highly articulate one.

As well as expressing his own emotional state, Van Gogh's art also tells us a great deal about the events of his life, since everything that happened to him was directly reflected in his subjects and how he painted them. This again makes him very approachable, an artist who keeps nothing hidden from his audience. However, the expression of his thoughts and feelings, and the description of events in his life were not confined to his paintings. Throughout his life he recorded his intimate thoughts in a remarkable series of letters to his brother Theo, who worked as an art dealer in Paris. The two brothers were extremely close, sharing similar temperaments and concerns. Published after Theo's death, this correspondence tells the same story as the paintings, of the many false starts in life, of his struggle for survival as a painter and of his mental collapse and periodic internments in a lunatic asylym. Through these intimate and moving letters it is possible to know Van Gogh as closely as his own brother did, and to follow the struggle of his life and the development of his art.

Background and early life

Van Gogh's life reflected many of the central issues of his time, in particular religion and socialism, the two great formative influences on his life, which were also of crucial importance in the history of the nineteenth century itself. He was the son of a Dutch Protestant minister, and throughout his early life he idolized his father and was himself deeply devout. He began his career, however, following in the footsteps of his uncle Vincent, who had been an important figure in the firm of Goupil & Co., picture dealers with branches in Paris, London and The Hague. Van Gogh worked for short periods at all three of these branches, but after seven years of increasing disillusionment both with his employers and with the business itself, he left, at the age of twenty-three.

He then traveled to England and taught for a while, first at a boy's school on the south coast and then on the outskirts of west London. During this time he became more and more absorbed in the idea of an ascetic way of life and in mystical, evangelical Protestantism. He decided to return to Holland to train for the ministry at a college in Amsterdam, but left after barely a year, disheartened by the need to study for what he saw as irrelevant academic exams. He decided to move to Brussels, where he enrolled in an evangelical missionary college, but managed to alarm the authorities with the extreme fervor of his convictions. After three months he was sent to preach amongst the miners of the Borinage region, but was dismissed for the excessive zeal with which he embraced and emulated the poverty of his surroundings. The intensity with which he approached life drove him to take his religious beliefs to what seemed their logical conclusion, and his desire to lead a life of poverty based on Christ's own at the expense of the usual social or religious conventions led to a parting of the ways with his superiors. By the time when, as a struggling painter in The Hague, he had set up house with a prostitute whom he hoped to save from her former ways, he had quite broken away from the conventional morality of the established Protestant church, and later, when he left Holland for Paris, he even abandoned his belief in God. His early years as a devout Christian, however, were to remain with him in his painting, as was the deeply moral standpoint from which he viewed the world, evidenced by his choice of the poorest of society as his subjects. The

JEAN FRANÇOIS MILLET
The Angelus
1857-9, Musée d'Orsay, Paris

This is typical of Millet's simple and dramatic compositions, many of which feature poorly clad figures set against a stark landscape. The religious element of the picture, however, produces a note of sentimentality lacking from many of his more defiant depictions of peasant hardship, which had a profound influence of Van Gogh.

VINCENT VAN GOGH
The Blacksmith
1882, Private collection

This charcoal drawing dates from the period Van Gogh spent in The Hague, when he was influenced by the realistic style and subject matter of the Hague School of painters. He produced many drawings and lithographs at this time, before his love of color was awakened.

manner in which he sacrificed all else to work as a painter also recalled his early life, and he himself compared his life to that of a monk, who lives only for his vocation.

In abandoning a Christian answer to the injustice and suffering of his times, Van Gogh drew closer to a more political stance. Although he was at no time directly involved in the political turmoil of the age, in which socialism was fast developing as a major force, he made it plain, both in his letters to Theo and in his paintings, where his sympathies lay. Even when staying in the relative comfort of his father's parsonage at Neunen after the failure of his attempt to make a career as an artist in The Hague, it was the poor weavers and the farm laborers that he drew. His plans for producing art together with his fellow artists mirrored the socialist ideal for society as a whole. While in The Hague he had developed a scheme whereby he and like-minded fellows would work as a co-operative, mass-producing cheap lithographic prints for the working class. The idea was that all the artists would work with no thought for personal gain, and if the business dissolved the remaining prints would be distributed free. In Paris, where socialist and anarchist views were common among his painter friends, he continued to dream of communities of painters working together.

VINCENT VAN GOGH
Peasant Head
1884, Private Collection

Van Gogh's intense sympathy for the poor is clearly shown in this portrait. The dark tones and muddy color are typical of his Dutch work, the most famous example of which is *The Potato Eaters* (see page 23). Studies such as this were among the preparations for the painting.

VINCENT VAN GOGH
Sorrowing Old Man
1890, Kröller-Müller Museum, Otterlo

Van Gogh first drew this subject in Holland, but he produced this version in the last year of his life. By this time it had become for him an image of both universal human suffering and the pain of his own life.

The new realism

Van Gogh's drift from radical evangelicism to a secular concern for social issues mirrored the broader issues of the times, notably the shift from the great religious revival of the nineteenth century to the social turmoil of the twentieth. Other artists and writers as sensitive as Van Gogh were moving in the same direction as the nineteenth century drew to a close, Leo Tolstoy's development in terms of social conscience being much of a parallel to Van Gogh's own, although the two never met. The literature of the time sheds valuable light on the influences that helped to form Van Gogh's painting, and the artist was himself extremely well read. A simple, eloquent statement of the role of religion and contemporary literature in his life is given in a painting he produced after his father's death, depicting the large family bible placed next to an extinguished candle. In the foreground is a novel by the French realist writer Emile Zola, a symbol of the future course of Van Gogh's life.

In his correspondence he continually refers to novels by such writers as Jean Michelet, the Goncourt brothers, Zola, Charles Dickens and Victor Hugo, and he saw the common thread between these writers as being the determined, often aggressive, realism with which they depicted contemporary life, particularly the sufferings of the poorer classes. Many of Van Gogh's favorite painters were those who shared his close relationship with literature, who actually worked as illustrators, or who shared the same devotion to realism that he saw in his

CAMILLE PISSARRO
Sunshine at Rouen
1896, Private collection

Pissarro's kindly nature made him the most approachable of the original members of the Impressionist group. Van Gogh was not the only artist to owe him a debt; he also taught Gauguin and Cézanne how to capture the colors of outdoor light using small dabs of paint, as in this typical painting.

favorite writers. From his own Dutch heritage he admired Rembrandt in particular for the humanity and sensitivity he brought to his Biblical scenes, and the French artist Honoré Daumier (1808-79) struck a chord in Van Gogh for the way he had ridiculed the establishment in his popular engravings. Toward the end of his life, when he had committed himself to the asylum at St Rémy and his choice of subject matter was necessarily limited, Van Gogh produced his own versions of the work of both these artists.

In his emphasis on visual, as well as social, realism, Van Gogh can be seen as belonging to the central tradition of Dutch painting. Since the seventeenth century Dutch painters had chosen their subjects from everyday life, and in the mid-nineteenth century these themes had been given a further significance by The Hague School of painters, led by Josef Israels. Although deeply rooted in the traditions of their own country, these painters were also part of the Realist movement in painting that was current throughout mid-nineteenth century Europe. This had started in France where it became the focus of opposition to the Academy, which exerted almost complete control over the style and content of French painting through the monopoly held by its own exhibitions. The Realists, by creating small, pioneering, alternative exhibitions, were able to challenge the conservative Academy and its promotion of historical, mythological and religious subject matter as the only concerns of the serious painter. The Realist painters depicted ordinary working people, often in the fields, and painted the French landscape as they saw it, often working directly from life in the open air, rather than constructing highly embellished studio pieces from sketches as the Academicians did. There were precedents for such innovations in Dutch and English painting, but in France the Realists saw themselves as revolutionaries, and they established the notion of an artistic avant-garde — young painters suffering poverty rather than compromising their style.

CLAUDE MONET
Evening at Argenteuil
1872, Private Collection

A typical river scene by the master of the Impressionist landscape. Monet painted on the spot to capture the exact colors that made up shadows in particular light conditions. He was particularly drawn to the surface of water as a subject that encouraged him to break up distracting details.

The Realists not only rejected the outmoded, idealized and escapist subjects of the Academicians but also the genteel polish they gave to their paintings. One of the leading Realist artists, Gustave Courbet (1819-77), delighted in exploiting the range of textures available with oil paints, and refused to disguise the vigorous brushwork he used to achieve his effects. The vitality and freedom of this sort of painting was to influence many later artists, Van Gogh among them.

But the Realist painter Van Gogh admired above all others was François Millet (1814-75). The hardship of Millet's life was similar to Van Gogh's own; from peasant stock himself, Millet had rejected a career in Paris to live among the peasants, and his pictures were deliberately stark, somber and crude. He gave his peasant subjects, often only a single figure set against a bare, uninviting landscape, a grandeur and dignity quite unprecedented in art history, so that they frequently appeared as heroic, grandiose figures, seemingly far removed from the physical hardship of their lives. Van Gogh loved the simplicity and power of these pictures, and he also found the religious overtones of many of them sympathetic. He was later to comment that although Millet, like himself, was steeped in the Bible, he never chose to paint directly religious subjects, but instead expressed his natural piety through the real world around him and the way he painted it. An aim which was precisely Van Gogh's own.

VINCENT VAN GOGH
A Corner of a Park
1888, Pen and ink drawing
Private collection

During his early months in Arles, Van Gogh used a reed pen in imitation of the Japanese masters. This drawing shows the large vocabulary of different strokes he had at his command, derived from the new knowledge he had acquired in Paris, and it demonstrates the same interest in varied textures and surfaces as his later paintings.

By the 1800s, when Van Gogh began to paint seriously, Millet was dead, but his reputation was established and his works had become popular and widely known through the circulation of engravings. Paris was now the center of avant-garde painting in Europe, and the modern movement set in motion by the Realists had moved far beyond the work of Millet. Van Gogh's brother Theo, who was now working in Paris for Goupil, wrote to tell his brother of the new generation of Realist painters, the Impressionists, and to describe their views of the city and countryside. Without having seen their work, however, Van Gogh was unable to comprehend their significance, and remained absorbed by Millet.

The Impressionists and after

It was not until he joined Theo in Paris in 1886 that he actually saw the work of Monet, Renoir, Degas and Pissarro and realized what the Impressionists had achieved. Building on the same foundations as the Realists, and painting much the same subjects, they had begun to concentrate much more on color and the effects of natural light than on the precise details of the scenes before them. Their palettes became ever lighter and of ever purer colors as they systematically banished the black pigment that had traditionally controlled the tonality of a picture, and began reproducing the hues they saw in nature. Under the influence of the Impressionists, Van Gogh's painting underwent a dramatic change, from the dark and somber colors of his Dutch work to the new vividness of the French landscape style. For a while he

Opposite page
GEORGES SEURAT
Bathing, Asnières
1884, National Gallery, London

The surface of this work is made up of countless tiny brushstrokes of differing colors that merge, when seen at the usual distance, into the subtle hues of a sunlit outdoor scene. Van Gogh was influenced by Seurat and his followers.

Opposite page
HOKUSAI
Temma Bridge at Osaka
c 1830, Victoria and Albert Museum, London

Van Gogh loved the brilliant, pure colors he saw in the work of Japanese printmakers such as Hokusai. Japanese art had been a major influence on the Impressionists for the same reason, and had a large following among Paris artists.

GEORGE SEURAT *Bathing, Asnières*

HOKUSAI *Temma Bridge at Osaka*

painted the Impressionist subject matter of parks and riverside scenes, with the same broken brushwork and pure colors, indeed the discovery of bright, sunny colors was a revelation to him and he continued to use them almost until his death. However, he had soon absorbed all that the Impressionists could teach him – they were now becoming rather remote and successful figures – and found himself facing new challenges.

PAUL GAUGUIN
Van Gogh Painting Sunflowers
1888

Gauguin has depicted Van Gogh painting one of his favorite subjects. While Van Gogh used Impressionist brushwork as a starting point to develop his own more expressive form, Gauguin soon rejected it altogether to concentrate on expressing his poetic and visionary ideas through flatly painted areas of color.

As Impressionism became an established style taught by its creators, particularly Camille Pissarro, to younger artists such as Van Gogh, its limitations became clearer. To record contemporary life in its true sunlit colors no longer seemed a compelling task for the avant-garde, but for this new generation, later to be known as the Post-Impressionists, the way forward was not immediately clear. Some became followers of Georges Seurat, who was attempting to create a new form of Impressionism, Pointillism, based on the scientific observation of light and tiny, uniform brushstrokes of pure color. For a while Van Gogh painted with Paul Signac, an ardent convert to Seurat's style, but others, like Paul Gauguin and Emile Bernard, began to turn away from the depiction of mundane reality altogether and to seek objects in religion, mythology or far-away, exotic places.

VAN GOGH'S PAINTING METHODS

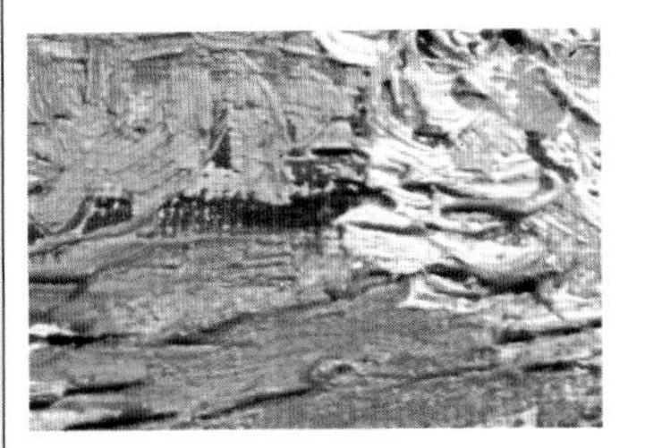

In this detail from Peach Trees in Blossom *the cream-beige of the canvas priming is just visible between the thickly impasted brushstrokes.*

Here, in the painting Hospital Garden at St Rémy, *the brushstrokes describe the form of the tree and suggest the rough texture of the bark.*

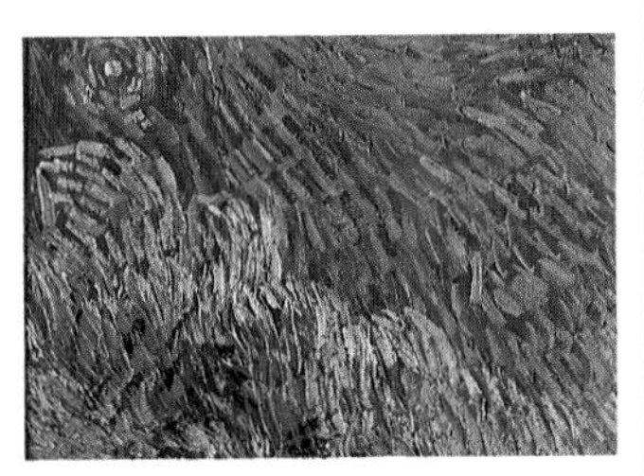

In the sky area of Road with Cypress and Star *the brushstrokes are expressionistic, giving a feeling of restlessness and turbulence.*

For the Impressionists, color was a vital means of conveying optical effects, but for Van Gogh and his successors, the Expressionists, it was much more than that. For these artists, painting was a whole language, in which line and color were called upon to interpret feelings and a personal vision. Van Gogh claimed to be able to express "those terrible things, men's passions" by red and green, and he saw certain colors, juxtapositions and contrasts as having their own symbolic significance. In a letter of 1888 he described an intention "to express the love of two lovers by a marriage of two complementary colors, their mingling and their opposition, the mysterious vibration of kindred tones."

The way he used paint was very personal and equally expressive, the result of much conscious experimentation as well as an instinctive feeling for the creation of a varied paint surface. In his later works he used his bright, vibrant colors in thick, rich impastos, with brushstrokes that echoed the forms of the subject, often working wet-into-wet so that the colors were slurred together, but sometimes dragging dry, thick paint over an already dry underlayer or working in a crisscross pattern of strokes. He liked a matt surface, and both he and Gauguin experimented with coarse, unprimed canvas such as hessian, which absorbs the oil binding from the paint. The majority of his paintings, however, are on ready-primed canvas which he bought in rolls and stretched himself. The grounds he preferred were off-white, gray, white or warm pink, and in some paintings the ground colors are allowed to show through.

In his mature works of the Arles period, such as Chair with Pipe, *Van Gogh used the small but vivid palette shown here, with lead white and some earth colors.*

1 Red lake; 2 Vermilion; 3 Cadmium yellow; 4 Ultramarine; 5 Cobalt blue; 6 Cobalt violet; 7 Emerald green; 8 Viridian

The path to self-expression

Although Van Gogh adopted the color and brushwork of the Impressionists his whole background and character distanced him from their approach. Working with Pissarro or Signac had been essentially part of his artistic education – catching up with the developments in Paris – but he was temperamentally unsuited to making pictures that were dispassionate visual records, and having extended his own technical range he was once again ready to make his own personal statements. He always looked for subjects that had a special significance to him, often a deeper one than their mere appearance, and after he had left Paris in 1888 to paint in the south of France his work became more and more personal, echoing the increasingly turbulent events of his life.

Van Gogh thus became one of the leading figures of Post-Impressionism, building on the work of the Impressionists but moving forward in a totally new direction, and the Post-Impressionist "alternative" that he developed in the last two years of his life was to become one of the most important paths to be followed by painters of the twentieth century. Although still taking his inspiration from the scene before him, his interpretation of it became far freer. The relationship between artist and subject assumed an equality, the artist imposing his own feelings on his subject in a way that had not been done before, by simplifying forms, distorting perspective and altering colors. All this was carried out with brushwork of such vigor and paint of such thickness that the viewer is constantly reminded of the painting's nature as an object with its own flat surface, rather than seeing it as a window through which a "real" scene is perceived. As his mental state became more precarious – from December 1888 onwards he suffered periodic attacks of insanity and had to spend time in the hospital at Arles and the asylum of St Rémy – his technique became increasingly concerned with self-expression rather than the strict recording of visual impressions.

Opposite page
VINCENT VAN GOGH
Sunflowers
1889, Private Collection

Van Gogh painted several versions of this favorite subject, which seemed to him the very essence of the bright sun of the south of France.

EDVARD MUNCH
Dream Self-Portrait
c 1926, Private collection

Like Van Gogh, Munch explored his inner anguish through a long series of self-portraits. He developed the expressionist elements of Van Gogh's later work to produce pictures that were characterized by a highly subjective use of color and distortion of space.

Van Gogh's heritage

Van Gogh sold only one painting in his lifetime, but his suicide at Auvers, near Paris, in July 1890, coincided with a time when his work was becoming better known and appreciated, at least by his fellow artists. As his fame grew his work appeared in exhibitions throughout Europe, and his influence became discernible in the work of others. It was in northern Europe that his paintings were perhaps best understood. The Norwegian Edvard Munch (1863-1944) shared something of Van Gogh's emotional make-up, for he himself suffered from deep depressions and led a life scarred by trauma. Munch began to employ similar distortions of space and color with expressive brushwork to communicate emotional states. The two artists' backgrounds and concerns were similar enough to suggest that in some respects Munch, who became an important influence on German twentieth-century art, continued Van Gogh's work, thus establishing a thread running right through to the present century. This thread brought a need to describe the new kind of painting, and the term which came to be used, Expressionism, was particularly attached to two groups of German painters working before the First

World War, *Die Brücke* ("The Bridge") of Dresden and *Der Blaue Reiter* ("The Blue Rider") of Munich. Although different in style both from each other and from their forebears, these two groups of artists owed their freedom to express themselves directly and non-descriptively to Van Gogh, who came to be viewed with hindsight as the father of modern Expressionism. This has been a recurring theme in modern painting: it emerged, revitalized, in American painting of the 1940s and '50s as Abstract Expressionism, with Van Gogh again acknowledged as the original inspiration. A sequence of books and exhibitions from this time confirmed his status, and the English master Francis Bacon (b.1909) produced a series of paintings derived from Van Gogh's own self-portrait of *The Artist Going to Work* as a direct homage.

Today, a hundred years after Van Gogh's revolutionary paintings in the south of France, modern painting in Europe and America has returned to a form of Expressionism, vigorously and often violently produced but nevertheless recognizable as descending from the same source. Van Gogh himself has become a symbol to the world of the artist struggling to make sense of the pain and hardship that he saw as the human condition. Through his life and work he brought the painter's role to its moral peak as one who works for his fellow man as interpreter of his hopes and as comforter for his suffering. His struggle to express himself through his painting has come to represent modern man's struggle to make sense of a hostile and confusing world.

FRANCIS BACON
Study for Portrait of Van Gogh VI
1957, Arts Council of Great Britain

This work is a tribute to Van Gogh by the contemporary English artist Francis Bacon, based on a Van Gogh painting of himself walking to work.

Opposite page
VINCENT VAN GOGH
The Garden of the Asylum at St Rémy
1889, Musée d'Orsay, Paris

In his later works the turmoil of Van Gogh's mind becomes the principal subject of his paintings. Here it is clearly seen in the charged brushwork with which the tree is painted. A disturbing note is added by the faceless figure standing in the foreground, thought to be the director of the asylum.

CHRONOLOGY OF VAN GOGH'S LIFE

1853 March 30th: Vincent Van Gogh born in the parsonage of Groot Zundert, Holland.

1869 Joins Goupil & Co., art dealers, in The Hague.

1873-5 Works for Goupil in London and Paris.

1876 Schoolmaster in England.

1877 Studies in Amsterdam for the entrance exam to the Theological Seminary.

1878 July: gives up his studies in Amsterdam and enters evangelical school in Brussels. December: sent to preach in the mining district of the Borinage, Belgium.

1879 Dismissed from his post but continues to work nearby.

1880 Starts drawing and attends art classes in Brussels.

1881 Working at The Hague, taught by the painter Anton Mauve.

1882 Living in The Hague with a prostitute and her child.

1883 September: moves to Drenthe in east Holland to paint the peasants.

Portrait of Père Tanguy

Road with Cypress and Star

1885 September-October: paints *The Potato Eaters.* November: moves to Antwerp.

1886 January: attends the Academy of Art in Antwerp. February: moves to Paris.

1887 *Kitchen Gardens in Montmartre. Portrait of Père Tanguy.*

1888 February: leaves Paris for Arles. October: arrival of Gauguin at Arles. November: *Vincent's Chair with his Pipe. L'Arlesienne.* December: first mental collapse.

1889 January: *Self-portrait with Bandaged Ear.* Further break-downs – enters hospital at Arles. May: Moves to the mental asylum at St Rémy. *Road with Cypress and Star.*

1890 May: briefly visits Paris and moves to Auvers-sur-Oise.
June: *Portrait of Dr Gachet.*
July: *Crows in the Wheatfield.*
July 27th: shoots himself, but misses his heart.
July 29th: dies at Auvers.

Paul Gachet, *Van Gogh on His Deathbed*, 1890, Louvre, Paris

The Paintings

The Potato Eaters

1885
$32^1/_4 \times 45$in/82×114cm
Oil on canvas
Van Gogh Museum, Amsterdam

The Potato Eaters was painted toward the end of a period of relative stability in Van Gogh's life. After the difficult time at The Hague, when his first efforts at working as an independent artist with his own studio had been undermined by the stress of setting up a household with his ex-prostitute lover and her child, he made a brief stay in the bare, rainswept heathland around Drenthe in eastern Holland and then, in 1883, returned to live with his parents at Neunen in Brabant. The last time Van Gogh had lived with his parents he had stormed out to move to The Hague, but now, although he acknowledged to Theo that there were still tensions between them, both sides endeavored to avoid actual conflict. Tending an illness of his mother with the same care that he had given to influenza-stricken miners in the Borinage showed his father a different side of his character and helped to draw them together.

He worked hard at his painting while at Neunen and progressed rapidly. *The Potato Eaters* draws together all that he had observed about peasant life in his early years, using the new skills he developed in The Hague. The dark interior recalls the many studies he made of the weavers of Neunen toiling over huge, creaking looms in cramped, poorly lit rooms, and the faces of the family are not direct portraits but a sort of composite, deriving from the many studies of heads he produced at this time. These, like those in *The Potato Eaters*, were painted with deliberately crude strokes, not because Van Gogh was in any way inept in the use of paint, but because he was trying to convey what he saw as the very essence of their way of life. He said himself that he would like to produce paintings of peasant life that looked as if they had been painted with the very soil of the fields.

Although firmly rooted in real social conditions, the painting has a further dimension. The simple dignity of the scene has been likened to a painting of a religious ceremony, even to a Last Supper. Such an impression is given validity by the fact that when asked by a neighbor — an amateur painter — to decorate his dining room with religious scenes Van Gogh preferred to produce scenes from peasant life, including a meal of potatoes.

Throughout this period Van Gogh produced a large number of charcoal drawings, using dark, strong strokes. Although his main interest was still the figure, these drawings also show a strong interest in the effects of chiaroscuro, or light and shade, as does *The Potato Eaters*, which was produced as a lithographic print as well as a painting. Although a dark painting it is not completely reliant on tonality, and even the deepest shadows have color. Van Gogh was able to produce extremely vital "muddy" tones by mixing a number of pigments together to produce variations of dark, neutral colors instead of simply using dark brown or black, which produce a lifeless effect. When blue and shades of brown (in this case raw and roasted sienna) are mixed together they give a luminous and atmospheric near-black, to which blues, yellows and reds can be added to gain the required variations.

The Potato Eaters is typical of Van Gogh's Dutch interiors in its use of a very few bright highlights against a predominantly dark background. Throughout his career Van Gogh was particularly aware of the dramatic possibility of strong contrasts in his paintings, but as his talent and knowledge of painting developed these contrasts were focused less around light and dark than around cool and warm colors, foreground and background, different textures of paint and so on. It has been suggested that these recurring pictorial tensions and oppositions may help to reveal something about the inner conflicts from which he suffered.

In this case the murky interior is intended to stress the poverty and hardship of the peasants' lives, but the occasional highlights also help to create a feeling of attractive intimacy – the sort of simple fellowship that Van Gogh himself craved.

1

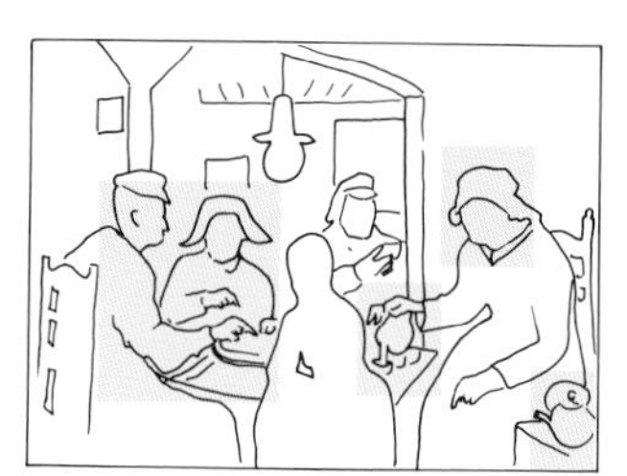

1 The apparent crudity of the brushstrokes belies the accuracy and economy of their use. The veins and knuckles of the hands, for instance, are treated with much more care than is seen on the sketches which led up to this work, such as the *Peasant Head* (see page 8). Van Gogh viewed this painting as a major work and devoted his most concentrated skill to it.

2 A sparing use of half-tones creates the very strongly molded face of the peasant woman. The darkest area of her cap demands a correspondingly lighter "halo" of wall behind to create the silhouette. Looser, thinner paint is used for the background to help push the figure forward — again reminding us of Rembrandt's work, where the thinnest paint is in the background.

3 The subtlety of Van Gogh's handling of tone is shown in the form of the pot, lightly painted in an area of what appears to be deep shadow, almost lost against the highlights of the central area. It is also possible to see how the shading is created by a mix of different colors, not a pure black or dark brown.

4 *Actual size detail* Here Van Gogh "draws" with the brush to create the form of the coffeepot with a few directional strokes. The same technique is used on the hands, the painter's concern being more with the texture of his own paint than with those of the surfaces he is depicting.

2

3

4 *Actual size detail*

Kitchen Gardens in Montmartre

Summer 1897
37¾×47¼in/96×120cm
Oil on canvas
Van Gogh Museum, Amsterdam

Van Gogh arrived in Paris to stay with his brother in February 1886, and at last he was able to see at first hand the work of the artists whom Theo had praised so highly in his letters. Seeing his first Impressionist paintings was the greatest revelation to him, for no amount of written description could have prepared him for the surprise and delight of discovering the purity of their colors. The heavy, expressive shading that he had used so effectively to evoke the poverty and drudgery of Dutch peasant life began to vanish, and like the Impressionists he began to use far less black in his palette, and to concentrate more on landscape painting than on figures.

The apartment he shared with Theo was on the slopes of Montmartre, on the very edge of the city and dominated by the Moulin de la Galette, the original windmill, standing above the more recent dance hall. Beyond were the sheds and smallholdings that blurred the boundary between city and open countryside. Typically Van Gogh chose this area as the subject for several landscapes, just as earlier he had shunned the picturesqueness of The Hague's old buildings to paint the outlying more modern ones. Although his paintings were now more attractively colored he still resisted the lure of the conventionally pretty or the familiar for his subject matter.

The founding fathers of Impressionism, whom Van Gogh admired so greatly, were remote figures to him in personal terms, the painters he met and worked with being the less well established, younger ones. Among these was Paul Signac, the enthusiastic disciple of Georges Seurat and follower of Seurat's Pointillist style – so called because it attempted to regulate Impressionism by the use of tiny point-sized brushstrokes to control precisely the accurate depiction of color. Here Van Gogh's debt to the technique can be seen clearly, yet the effect he creates is one of movement rather than a calm uniformity of brushstroke. He has ignored Seurat's scientific theories, and used his own version of Pointillism to create an exciting surface pattern.

Here Van Gogh conveys an impression of the exhilaration of open space so near the crowded city by the dramatic movement of his foreground path which pushes forcefully into the middle ground. A series of parallel diagonals of paths and fences echo this movement, pointing both toward the distance and toward a remarkably freely rendered area of color in the righthand corner of the landscape. This constitutes a near-abstract celebration of the pure color he had discovered in Paris. From the freshness of these colors it is easy to sense that the work was painted in the open air, in the Impressionist manner, and the openness of the brushwork, through which bare canvas is often visible, creates the illusion of space and light entering the painting.

1

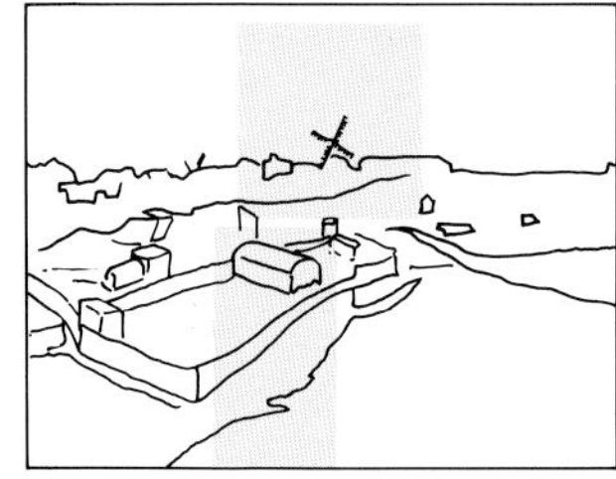

1 The dense dots of the Pointillist style that Van Gogh had seen in the work of Seurat and the younger artist Signac are used only sparingly, as in the wall of the background shed. They are only a part of a pattern of various different strokes used here with a freedom and a lightness of touch new in Van Gogh's work.

2 The thinner and paler paint of the sky toward the horizon suggest recession into space (atmospheric perspective), but are confidently offset by the pure color of the windmill's sails and the roof of the distant shed.

2

Portrait of Pere Tanguy

Autumn 1887
$36^1/_4 \times 29^1/_2$in/92×75cm
Oil on canvas
Musée Rodin, Paris

Close to the apartment Van Gogh shared with his brother in Paris was "Père" ("Father") Tanguy's shop, an important meeting place for avant-garde painters. Tanguy sold artists' materials, and often used to exchange them for finished works from impecunious young painters, in time building up a large stock of works of art. His shop became a place to see the work of other artists and to exchange ideas on style and technique. The comradeship thus provided appealed to Van Gogh's longing for a sense of community between painters and, more than this, he found he and Tanguy had a strong mutual rapport. Tanguy was a man of humble origins with left-wing political convictions, who had been deported and served two years hard labor for his part in the Paris Commune of 1871. On returning to Paris he had made a living touring the suburbs selling paints to the young artists working there – the future Impressionists – and Camille Pissarro had later helped him to set up his own shop.

Besides modern painting Tanguy also sold Japanese prints, and this portrait is as much about these as it is about the sitter himself. Japanese art was still a relatively new discovery in the west. Van Gogh had first encountered it in Antwerp, but it was in Paris that he became almost obsessive about the bold design and, above all, the pure, strong colors of these prints. He made copies of Japanese prints, organized an exhibition of them in a café, and was allowed a free range around the largest oriental art showroom in Paris. He associated the vividness of color in these prints with the bright sunlight of the Orient, and his craving for this vividness led him to leave Paris to search for his own version of it in the south of France.

Van Gogh painted several portraits of Tanguy, one of which, in Athens, is almost identical to this one except that the Japanese prints in the background are in a different arrangement. In both portraits the brushwork has begun to look forward to that of his Arles period and the love of color is very obvious. From Arles, a year later, he wrote "A palette nowadays is absolutely colorful: sky blue, pink, orange, vermilion, strong yellow, clear green, pure wine red, purple."

Although it was the Impressionists who showed Van Gogh the use of pure colors, it was Seurat's work that taught him to look at color even more closely, and to analyze and separate the different hues that combined to make each area of color. In this portrait the blue of the jacket is composed of various hues of blue and other colors as well; one sees touches of red, green or orange among the very varied brushstrokes.

A particular lesson he learned was that of the value of complementary colors, those which are opposite one another on the "color wheel," and when placed in proximity appear more vivid. Blue and orange, and red and green are two such pairs, and both are used here. Touches of orange around the sitter set off the jacket, while the green strokes that represent the shadow of the upturned brim of his hat are interspersed with red.

1

2

1 At the time of this painting Japan was Van Gogh's ideal – a fantasy land of color, and in these copies of Japanese prints he could indulge his urge to break away from the constraints of realistic color. Here we see yellow houses and dabs of green snow, applied lightly with dabs of thin paint.

2 The painting clearly reveals the process of its creation, with the overlaid brushstrokes providing a history of the artist's methods. The brushstrokes on the face are very varied, those around the eyes and cheeks following the form, and the eyebrows and beard composed of short, jabbing strokes suggestive of texture.

3 *Actual size detail* The translucent quality of skin is superbly conveyed by the way the mustard yellow hues have been laid over the flesh tints. Veins are suggested by touches of blue, again making use of the interplay of complementaries. Below the hands the solidity of the sitter's legs is obscured under the urgent rush of brushstrokes; this amount of surface interest tends to flatten form.

3 *Actual size detail*

NIGHT CAFE

September 1888
27½×35in/69.8×88.9cm
Oil on canvas
Yale University of Art

Sleeping by day, Van Gogh produced this picture after three night's work. He described it as "one of the ugliest I have done," explaining that he had "tried to describe the terrible passions of humanity by means of green and red. Everywhere there is a clash and contrast of the most alien reds and greens." The landscapes that Van Gogh painted in Arles had something of the sunny innocence of the Impressionists, but this work is quite different, and in it he was returning to deeper concerns and conveying much more than superficial appearances. The infernal colors set in painful contrast to each other do indeed create an ugly picture, but they also transform the scene of a dingy café in the small hours of the night into a place of dread, fear and unhappiness. Unlike the Impressionists, Van Gogh wanted his pure colors to stir up a strong emotional reaction in the viewer.

It is not only the violent colors and crude brushstrokes that create the disturbing mood of the painting; the perspective is also dramatically exaggerated. The dimensions of the room are unsettling, with the floor seeming to rush away at our feet, and the possibility of escape through the curtained door seems distressingly distant. The size and position of objects and people are unsure, and familiar things seem distorted and threatening. In a dramatic contrast to the deep space Van Gogh has placed motifs that have an unnatural flatness, like cut-outs. The figure of the landlord, one of Van Gogh's creditors, stands in his white suit like an apparition, hovering behind his billiard table and fixing the painter with an unsettling gaze. The uniform thickness of the paint adds to the picture's atmosphere of heavy foreboding. Van Gogh himself said of the painting "I have attempted to show that the café is a place where a man can ruin himself, become mad, commit a crime . . ."

Van Gogh is most often remembered as a great colorist, but his use of a strong perspective is frequently an equally important element in his compositions. It was often exaggerated for expressive purposes, as in this and in many other of his later works, and the features of this painting, discussed above are in fact a register of the pictorial devices used by the Expressionist painter Munch and his successors.

A social scene such as this is rare in Van Gogh's work; more typically, such a comparatively large cast of figures is pushed to the back and sides of the picture and painted in a few summary strokes. Here the characters and appearance of the figures are less important to the painter than the distance which separates him from them. The casually placed chairs in the foreground recall a favorite device of the Impressionist painter Degas, but the bleakness of this gathering could not be further from the lively interest in personality apparent in Degas' work.

1

2

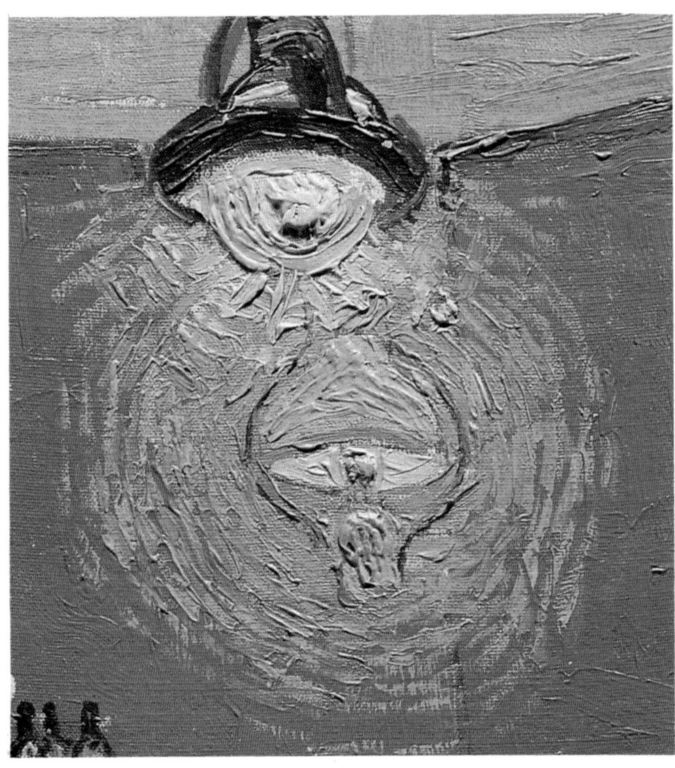

3

1 The uniform thickness of paint adds to the heavy atmosphere of the work. The body of paint left at the side and end of each stroke is best seen on the center table and the top of the neighboring stove, the latter being tilted up in accordance with the distorted perspective of the room.

2 The owner seems squeezed between the two tables, the unrelieved white of his suit helping to flatten him still further.

3 Increasingly separate strokes convey the incandescence of the lamp. Its center is green to bring it out from the surrounding red, another use of the opposition of complementaries seen in much of Van Gogh's work.

4 *Actual size detail* Rejecting distracting detail, Van Gogh has used the simplest movements of his brush to convey the fullness of the blooms and the somber congregation of bottles.

4 *Actual size detail*

L'Arlesienne

Arles November 1888
$35\frac{1}{2} \times 28\frac{1}{4}$in/$90 \times 71.7$cm
Oil on canvas
Musée d'Orsay, Paris

"Slashed on in an hour" is how Van Gogh described the production of this portrait of Madame Ginoux, words which are a vivid reminder of the intensity and speed with which he worked. His single-mindedness and energy were also noted by his contemporaries who remarked on his ability to sustain an output of one canvas a day working at full stretch; his obsession with certain subjects that would drive him out to paint them whatever the weather or time of day; and the paint-spattered clothes that resulted from his violent brushwork. But this portrait, despite the characteristic vivacity of the paint, gives a strong impression of calm and dignity. The sitter remains poised, yet the color scheme is one of brilliant drama – one of Van Gogh's most dashing fanfares of color.

The portrait's title derives from the sitter's dress: not a fanciful costume but the traditional clothes of a lady of Arles. In his letters Van Gogh frequently discussed how important it was for his sitters to dress in their ordinary clothes so that they appeared relaxed and assured, without the impersonal stiffness that handicapped more formal portraiture. As a portrait of a sympathetic neighbor, this painting is linked to his earlier *Père Tanguy* (see page 31), both being examples of the type of "democratic portraiture" that Van Gogh could be said to have created. Because he selected sitters who were simply friends and neighbors, with no worldly importance, he was freer to explore character and appearance than society portrait painters, who were often constrained by the necessity to convey social status in order to please their richer patrons. Van Gogh's portraits, indeed, were not done for money but as a mark of intimacy.

It was quite common for Van Gogh to paint a second version of a portrait he felt had been particularly successful, changing some minor details of dress, accessories or background. This he did with both *Père Tanguy* and *L'Arlesienne,* the alternative version of the latter including some open books, instead of a glove and umbrella, in front of the sitter. Gauguin also drew Madame Ginoux at this time, while he was staying with Van Gogh, and during his time in the asylum of St Rémy Van Gogh returned to this drawing, which he had kept, as the basis for a further painting.

Van Gogh manages to convey a natural grace and confidence in his sitter that help to make this work one of his more directly attractive portraits. Femininity is suggested, by the graceful curve of an eyebrow, for instance, but there is no superficial flattery, and the sitter's alert gaze gives a hint of a naturally intelligent and sympathetic nature. The pose itself is less expressive, for Van Gogh has concentrated upon the arresting color composition rather than establishing his sitter's position in the pictorial space more persuasively. There is an obvious debt to Gauguin here in the colors and the relative flatness of the forms.

1

2

1 For the background Van Gogh uses a variation of his blocked-in brushwork, with strong yellow horizontal strokes applied over fawn backing. The face itself is modeled in pale greens controlled by the slashes of stronger green on the shoulder, applied before the white beneath had dried. Yellow on the hand pushes it forward toward the viewer.

2 The painting of the umbrella and yellow flower-like shape on the red table top shows a marvelous use of the wet-into-wet technique. The paint is laid on very thickly but lightly so that it is modified by the colors below but not muddied by them. Here Van Gogh has again used his favorite complementaries — red and green — to create a glowing color harmony, enhanced by the cooling touches of blue in the green areas.

3 *Actual size detail* Here the texture of the canvas, evidently fairly coarse, is visible through the thinner layers of green-white paint. The flower on the bodice is built up in thick impasto, with the hint of pink in the white echoed in the brushstrokes surrounding it.

3 *Actual size detail*

VINCENT'S CHAIR WITH HIS PIPE

November 1888
$28^3/_4 \times 36^1/_4$in/73×92 cm
Oil on canvas
Tate Gallery, London

Van Gogh rented a small house in Arles, buying a respectable bed for the guest bedroom but furnishing his own room with the utmost simplicity. He painted a wide range of subjects during this time, including the room itself, and he described his plans for this picture to his brother. "This time it's just simply my bedroom, only here color is to do everything, and giving by its simplification a grander style to things, is to be suggestive here of rest or of sleep in general. In a word, to look at the picture ought to rest the brain or rather the imagination." A very succinct definition of the aim of his painting — the distillation of a spiritual quality from the most mundane reality.

The chair in this painting is identical to those from his bedroom that had appeared in the earlier work. As a subject it appears at first to be uncompromisingly ordinary, but in fact it is an eloquent parallel to the work and thoughts of a Japanese artist admired by Van Gogh, who devoted himself to the study of a single blade of grass, only to find that this seemingly simple task led him, step by step, to the contemplation of all that is in nature. By including his own pipe and tobacco on the seat Van Gogh connects the chair to its owner, and it thus begins to appear more as a kind of veiled self-portrait. He frequently painted the personal belongings that were particularly close to him — in Paris his battered boots, and in Arles his worn clogs — and these pictures tell us as much about the owner as they do about the objects themselves.

With this knowledge in mind it becomes obvious that the crudity of the drawing is deliberate, expressive rather than arbitrary, conveying the rough "earthenware" nature of both the south and of Van Gogh himself. He referred to this when he expressed the hope that one of his peasant portraits would be hung next to the glamorous, powdered Parisian artifice of a Toulouse-Lautrec work, so that both would be set off to their mutual advantage.

Opposite page
VINCENT VAN GOGH
Van Gogh's Bedroom at Arles
Van Gogh Museum, Amsterdam

The use of color and space in this view of Van Gogh's bedroom is extremely close to that seen in the painting of his own chair. Both paintings are reflections of his personality and way of life, almost forms of "self-portrait."

The color composition of this work is based on variations around the pairs of primary complementaries — blue and orange, and red and green. These appear in their purest form only in occasional passages, to set the keynotes for the composition. Thus the area of purest red on the paving beneath the chair is balanced by touches of green above it and by a further stroke of green on the nearest chair leg. Van Gogh stresses structure through emphatic outlines, added later, that serve to contain areas of pure painting. The strength of these increases the impact of the image but also creates a certain tension between line and color. In distorting the perspective of the floor and the chair leg, Van Gogh imposed his own personality upon the work, stressing the subjectivity of his view.

1

2

1 The pipe, handkerchief and tobacco give a focus to the picture in both narrative and pictorial terms, providing a note of neutral white at the center of the interplay of cool and warm hues. The use of blue to outline the parts of the chair increases the sense of cool draftsmanship restraining the sensuous handling of paint.

2 The floor tiles are painted with the weaving brushstrokes that Van Gogh often used in the backgrounds of his work at this time. Short horizontal and vertical strokes alternate in a loose mesh of reds, browns and greens. The thickness of the paint used is revealed by the heavy smear from the side of the brush that is left alongside each stroke.

3 *Actual size detail* The inconsistency of Van Gogh's finish can be seen here in the disparity between the caned seat of the chair, given considerable attention and depth of paint, and the sparsely painted top and edges of the chair leg. This adds to the variety and vivacity of the overall paint surface as well as telling us much about the speed with which he worked.

3 *Actual size detail*

Self-portrait with Bandaged Ear

January 1889
$23\frac{1}{2} \times 19\frac{1}{4}$ in/60×49 cm
Oil on canvas
Courtauld Institute Galleries, London

Over and over again Van Gogh returned to his own features as a subject, the number and variety of these self-portraits recalling those of his fellow-countryman Rembrandt. These works reflect both the loneliness of his life and his attitude toward himself and his circumstances; in them he was exploring what it was about himself that formed his unique view of the world and separated him from his fellows.

This is particularly true of this work, in which he presents his now famous bandaged ear to the viewer – himself – to draw attention to the self-mutilation rather than to hide it. There is thus an element of confession in the painting, as well as an urge to come to terms with a very damaging episode.

The severed ear was the climax to the eagerly anticipated visit to Arles of Paul Gauguin. Van Gogh had always hoped to found a community of painters working together and supporting each other artistically and emotionally, a microcosm of his dream of society. As a first step toward this ideal, he exchanged works with many of his colleagues – in imitation of the practice among the much-admired Japanese masters – and he had exchanged self-portraits with Gauguin through Theo in Paris. Now Gauguin had agreed to share Van Gogh's small house, motivated at least partly by the very poor state of his own finances and the knowledge that Van Gogh was being sent money by Theo.

The arrangement worked very well at first. Gauguin was stimulating, and knowledgeable, as well as being a very good cook, but it was not long before important artistic and personal differences began to surface. Both painters had just reached full artistic maturity, emerging from the shade of the Impressionists, but they had grown in different directions. Whereas Van Gogh had developed an extremely direct, emotional and expressive form of landscape painting, Gauguin's view of nature was much more artificial and his paintings incorporated imaginary elements, taken from religion, literature and his own memories. As the more confident and worldly of the two he was able to impose his views on Van Gogh, creating a distressing tension in the latter's work, which had previously been assured and tranquil.

Furthermore, Gauguin lacked Van Gogh's emotional delicacy in personal relations, and was soon encouraging the latter to join him in his frequent expeditions to the local brothels. The tension grew between the two, confined together in the small house, until finally it erupted and Van Gogh broke down, cutting off his ear and presenting it to a prostitute in the brothel. The furore this incident caused brought in the police, who removed Van Gogh to the local hospital, where he was to spend the majority of his time before transferring to the St Rémy asylum. Gauguin left for Paris, having prepared a mendacious version of the events to excuse his own involvement.

This portrait recalls the extreme isolation and depression that followed this affair. Van Gogh was left to absorb the terrible truth of his mental instability, and to confront the lowest ebb of his fortunes at a time when all appeared to have been going well. Thus we are presented with a haggard, shell-shocked figure, shabbily dressed and set against a background bare but for a Japanese print, an ironic reminder of the expectation of Japanese sunshine that had brought him to Arles.

The composition and execution of this self-portrait create the mood as strongly as does the artist's empty gaze. Behind him the easel, print and window appear disjointed, unrelated to each other. The space they occupy seems unclear: it is crowded and rather claustrophobic. On the coat, paint is applied in long, quick strokes pointing toward the face where the brushstrokes are laid in several conflicting directions. The heavily marked outlines no longer contain and counteract the overall restlessness of the surfaces, and although the pose is one of conventional stability — a triangle anchored on the two bottom corners of the picture — it seems to be in danger of imminent collapse from the agitated movement within it.

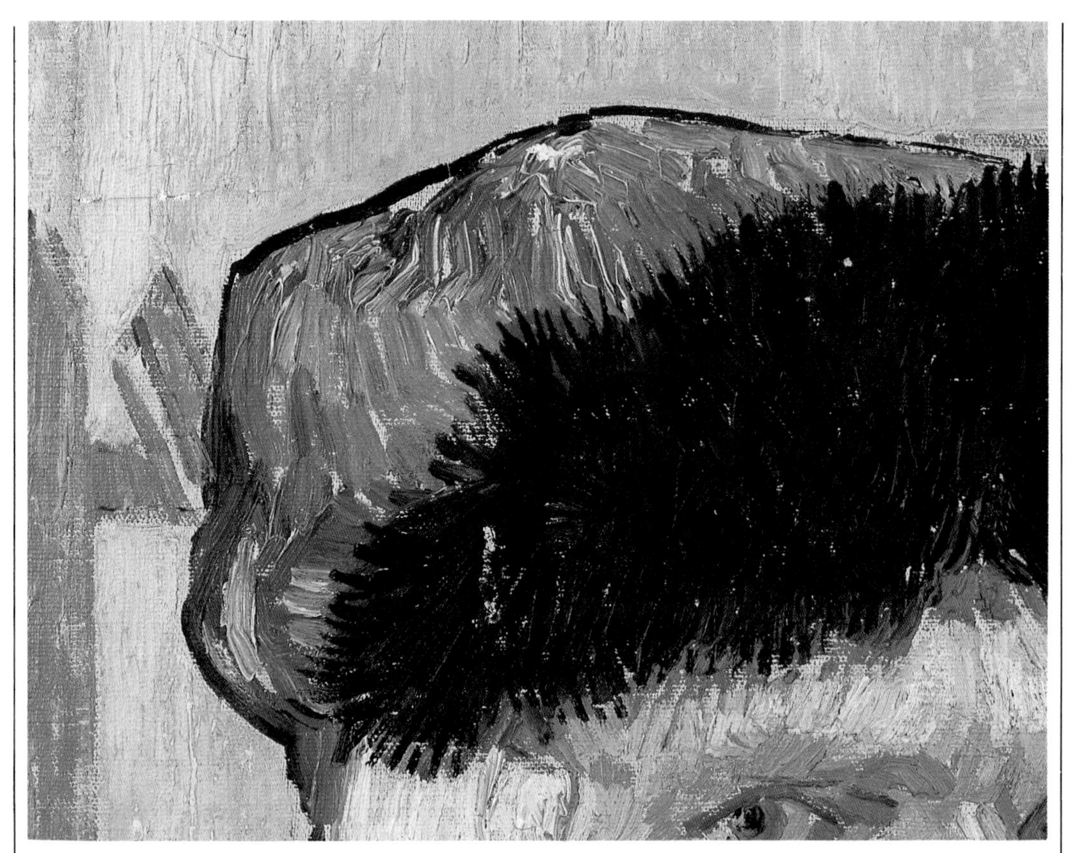

1

2

1 Toward the crown of the hat Van Gogh has used the conflicting zig-zag strokes that were to become more frequent in his later work. The outline fails to draw this movement together, nor has the painter tried to disguise the space left beneath it.

2 Few brushstrokes are alike in this area of the painting. Some are completed with the quick flick away at right-angles to the canvas that Van Gogh frequently used, which often resulted in small pinnacles of paint being left at the end of each rapid stroke.

3 *Actual size detail* The face is actually made up of a range of different colors — red eye-sockets, white lips and green chin — but the tonality is controlled with such assurance that it appears pale and drained when set against the rest of the picture. Bare canvas shows on the chin, but elsewhere the paint is thickly applied.

3 *Actual size detail*

Road with Cypress and Star

May 1890

36¼×28¾in/92×73cm

Oil on canvas

Rijksmuseum Kröller-Müller, Otterlo

At first Van Gogh had viewed his mental breakdown as the result of external circumstances: the emotional upheaval of Gauguin's visit, overwork and the effect of a poor diet with too much coffee, alcohol and tobacco. However, when he had a further attack, believing himself to be the victim of a poisoner, he was forced to acknowledge that the deeper cause lay within himself, and agreed to move to the asylum at St Rémy.

Here he quickly found that the asylum offered only simple internment rather than any active cure, but he accepted the conditions – the unpalatable food and demoralizing lack of activity – partly because his fits, sometimes violent, left him exhausted and listless for weeks afterward, and partly because he saw his stay in the asylum as a form of ascetic retreat, an austere foundation on which he hoped to reconstruct his life. He also admired the way the patients looked after one another, which echoed his own ideals of fellowship and community.

The exact nature of his illness has never been clear, though the two most plausible diagnoses are schizophrenia or a rare form of epilepsy accompanied by hallucinations. Between attacks he was still able to paint, and was even allowed to make short trips out to do so in the company of a warder. This painting, typical of his developing style, is quite different from his early work in Arles. Vigorous, troubled brushwork has returned, its movement creating restless and conflicting activity, and an expressionistic licence has appeared too, evident in the disturbing angle of the road and the travelers on it. The appearance of sun, moon and stars in his work at this time clearly shows how his search for the truth of what he saw was paradoxically leading him further away from realism toward a mystical vision reminiscent of the medieval world-view. His feeling for the south, associated with an Impressionist preoccupation with light, was changing too. He began to consider returning to northern Europe and, as his passion for the brilliant landscape waned his colors followed suit, becoming less bright and more diluted with half-tones. The image of the cypress tree, a mysterious evergreen link between heaven and earth, provided him with an opportunity to re-introduce into his work the deep, dark hues that had been absent since Holland.

It is the sense of urgency and agitation, not the subjects themselves, that makes Van Gogh's St Rémy landscapes so very remarkable. Here the composition seems to rush off in every direction from the pole of the cypress — to the left through the road, to the right with the rising clouds, and also upward, as the tree has been allowed to "bust" the frame at the top of the picture, which forces the viewer's eye to follow it. Every line of this composition is restless and undulating: each element buffets its neighbor, as the tide of the road rises to swamp the root of the cypress, or the breaking wave of the cornfield threatens to submerge it. The distant sky offers a little relief from these oppressive forces, but is itself turbulent with flowing, spiralling currents.

1

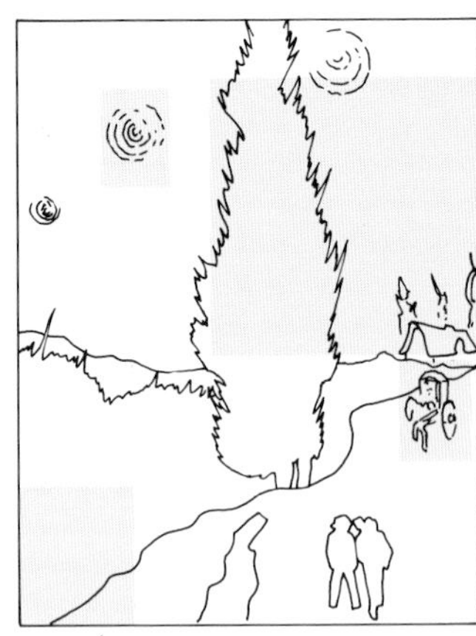

1 The ragged silhouette of the cypress contains a mass of short, angular, vigorous strokes made with a loaded brush. Deep blue helps to cool the dark greens even further, and is echoed in the distant trees, the only element that gives a sense of recession to the landscape.

2 Incongruous in scale, the cart is painted with untypical attention to detail, highlighting the freedom of the rest of the painting. The almost vertical strokes of the road seem to provide an unsure footing for the cart's journey.

3 Here Van Gogh has used less pure color, and in his haste, has allowed paint to mix before drying, as in the corn, thus losing some of the luminosity of his early work at Arles.

4 *Actual size detail* Van Gogh depicts the star as radiating yellow, green and white against the darkening sky. Below, short strokes collide and coalesce into awkward twisting movements.

2

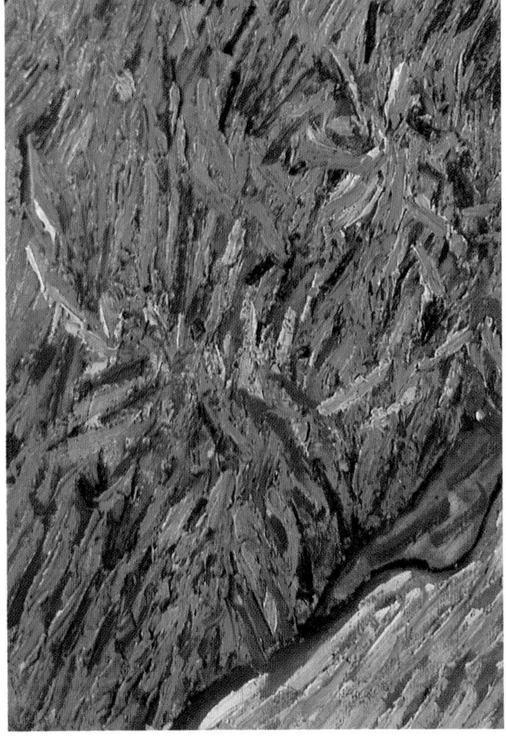
3

4 *Actual size detail*

Portrait of Dr Gachet

June 1890
26¾×22½in/68×57cm
Oil on canvas
Louvre, Paris

Van Gogh left the St Rémy asylum in May 1890. Since he was a voluntary patient he was free to leave when he wished, and he now felt ready to try to re-establish an independent life for himself. His stay there taught him no longer to fear mental abnormality and to view his own fits as an illness, as susceptible to treatment as any physical ailment. He spent a brief three days in Paris, where he impressed his brother, now married and with an infant son, with his health and good spirits, then left for Auvers, a small town near Paris, where he took a room at an inn.

Here he felt himself to be back in the north once more; in St Rémy he had begun to feel increasingly nostalgic for his homeland. The romance with the southern sun was over, and the more subdued grays, greens and browns that he had last used in Holland began to reappear in his landscapes. In the asylum he had re-examined the roots of his painting, in particular the great masters he had first admired, and he did this in a characteristically direct way, by painting his own versions of favorite works of which he possessed prints. This process helped to strengthen his confidence in his own work, which was becoming ever more personal.

The reason for the choice of Auvers was that it was the home of Dr Theo Gachet, who had agreed to act as Van Gogh's support there. Gachet, who was not just a doctor but a unique blend of the medical and the artistic, had long been connected with the Parisian avant-garde, and Cézanne and Pissarro were among the many painters who had visited him at Auvers. He had spent his youth frequenting the bohemian cafés of Paris and had known Courbet and Manet as well as the novelist Victor Hugo. As a socialist, republican, Darwinian and freethinker his outlook has been radical for its day, and now, in his middle age, he spent most of his time in his gloomy house among his antiques and modern pictures, practicing his hobby of etching. After the hectic events and bizarre company of St Rémy, Gachet was a welcome companion for Van Gogh, and one who shared his own views on painting. As always, the portrait is a testament of a friendship, for the artist felt a deep kinship for Gachet, whom he saw as a disappointed and isolated man. The pose he placed him in, with head resting on hand, is the traditional one of the melancholic, and Gachet's expression and the sadness of his eyes, the angle of his body and the claustrophobic, swaying background all combine to create a feeling of unease.

In mood the painting is unsettled and equivocal, but Van Gogh handles the sophisticated composition with assurance. *Père Tanguy* (see page 33) is seen frontally, while *L'Arlesienne* (see page 39) is placed slightly awkwardly in relation to the space around her, but here the sitter fills the canvas at a commanding diagonal to the almost square format. The pose is viewed slightly from above, as the sitter turns away from the painter, and the eye is drawn around in a circular movement through the arms and the connecting flower back again to the face. The contrasting diagonals – hard or undulating – of the table and background also focus on Gachet, so that the composition itself provides an active framework for the movement of Van Gogh's brush.

1

2

1 Van Gogh described the background as a landscape, but there is only the faintest suggestion of undulating hills against a sky. The essential contrast exists more in the brushwork itself, with rectilinear strokes set above longer touches of a more heavily loaded brush.

2 The painting of the cuff consists of simple brushstrokes applied on almost bare canvas. Underpainting has again been virtually abandoned in the immediacy of execution. Gachet's hand is drawn with a light, active line and thin paint, in contrast to the more worked surfaces on either side of it.

3 *Actual size detail* The solidity of the paint captures the almost tangible gathering of flesh folds as Gachet pushes his cheek upward with his fist. Touches of blue in the eyes and hand help to complement and heighten the ginger hair.

3 *Actual size detail*

Crows in the Wheatfield

Early June 1890
20×39½in/50.5×100.5cm
Oil on canvas
Van Gogh Museum, Amsterdam

Van Gogh was in good spirits when he arrived at Auvers, partly as a result of observing his brother's newfound domestic happiness, but when news reached him of financial troubles threatening Theo and his family he was thrown into dejection. Apart from the threat to his beloved brother, his own future was in question since he was on an allowance from Theo and his unhappiness was increased by a growing sense of guilt about his dependence on his brother and hence his role in Theo's misfortune. (There is evidence that this situation may have contributed to his first breakdown at Arles.) Now fear and guilt began to turn into depression, sometimes even violent rages, and he quarreled with Dr Gachet and was once again reduced to solitude. Although still lucid, he could sense the imminence of despair and madness, and he no longer felt able to fight against them.

He began to paint the great plain of wheatfields surrounding Auvers. When he had approached a similar subject from his window at St Rémy he had included the figure of the reaper, seen as a symbol of death advancing with his scythe, and now similar thoughts returned to him. He wrote of those wheatfield paintings that "They are vast stretches of corn under troubled skies, and I did not need to go out of my way to express sadness and the extreme of loneliness." In this version there is indeed a tangible sense of foreboding, as a flock of sinister black crows approaches in the vanguard of heavy, dark stormclouds. The road ahead is tilted up into an impossible incline and seems to peter out, offering no escape, while the brushwork is at its most expressionistic.

It was in these very fields that Van Gogh shot himself in the chest, and although he missed his target, his heart, and managed to drag himself back to the village where he collapsed into bed, he did not survive long. His landlord discovered him and summoned Theo from Paris to his brother's deathbed. "The sadness will last forever" were among the last words Theo heard him speak, and Theo himself, overcome with grief, died six months later.

Perhaps the most violently painted of Van Gogh's works, this is the epitome of a subjective, expressionist landscape. Every element of composition, color and brushwork is used in an attempt to arouse in the viewer the same emotions that possessed the artist as he worked. The landscape itself is devoid of any distracting incidents, completely lacking any human presence and with a bare, unrelieved horizon. Distance is extremely difficult to determine as the three tracks seem to be attempting unsuccessfully to scale an almost vertical slope. Nor is there any concern with conveying distance through atmospheric perspective – the color is uniformly intense, and the painting of the sky as thick as that of the foreground.

1

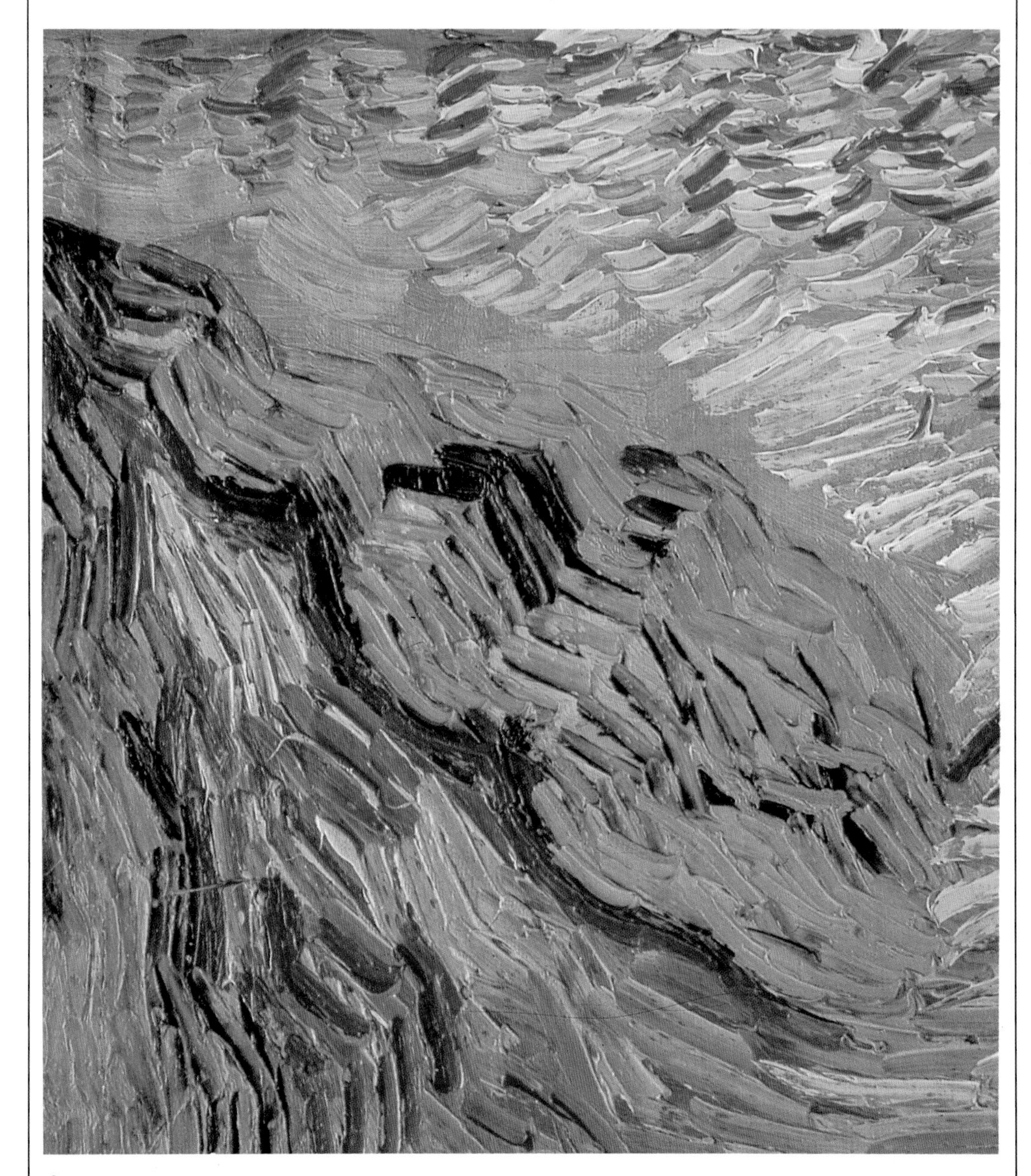

2

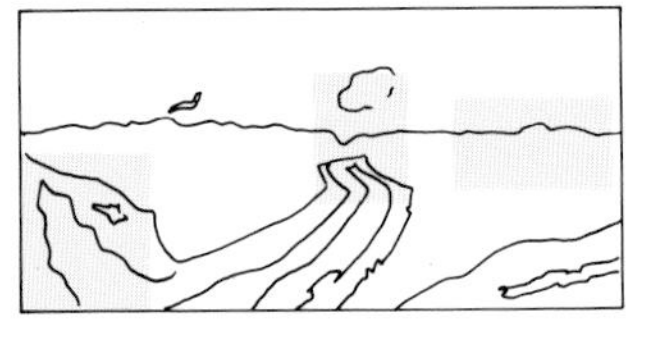

1 The dense mesh of short, rapid strokes that suggest the ears of corn blowing in the wind of the approaching storm are painted rapidly, wet-in-wet.

2 The livid colors used here reflect what Van Gogh felt, rather than what he saw. Darker tones are applied first, building up to lighter and brighter ones in a confused mass of shapeless movement.

3 *Actual size detail* There is no harmony in this painting, either in color or in brushwork; each stroke of the brush clashes with another so that the curves of the road consist of a series of tiny jagged angles. The same zig-zags represent the crows, reduced to the barest elements of the painter's "handwriting." Hues resembling blood and flesh are disturbingly present on the road beneath them.

3 *Actual size detail*

INDEX

Page numbers in *italic* refer to the illustrations and captions

PHOTOGRAPHIC CREDITS

The photographs in this book were provided by the following: Courtauld Institute Galleries, London 46-49; Hubert Josse, Paris 14, 20, 30-33, 38-41; National Gallery, London 13 top; National Museum Vincent Van Gogh, Amsterdam 26-29; Walter Rawlings, London 6, 42; Rijksmuseum Kröller-Müller, Otterlo 50-53; Saale Vorm & Uitgeefservice, Holland 22-25, 59-61; Tate Gallery, London 42-45; Victoria and Albert Museum, London 13 bottom; Visual Arts Library, London 7, 8 top and bottom, 11, 12, 17, 19.